Music Minus One Violoncello

Édouard Lalo

Violoncello Concerto in D minor

3780

TO THE CELLIST:

Here are a few words of advice on how to get the best use of the minus versions:

I would recommend playing along with the orchestra set at a fairly high volume for the first few attempts. With a certain amount of repetition it will be possible to familiarize yourself with the various tempi in different sections. This applies especially to the first movement since there are a few extended silences at the beginning, followed by three metronome taps that have been placed strategically just before cello solo entrances. It will take a little practice before you can predict how much time you will have to get through any section where the orchestra is silent.

The second and third movements are more straightforward and will present less of a challenge in this respect with the exception of the very opening of the third where an accent has been placed on the first and seventh eighth notes (beats one and three if each beat is thought of as a dotted quarter note.) This was necessary in order to offer an orientation for the cellist while the orchestra holds one note for six bars.

For these minus versions, we did not simply take the solo cello out and leave the orchestra as is. Instead we re-assessed each passage and picked tempi and tempo relations between passages that we thought would accommodate the most players. We have also boosted the volume and heightened the strength of the articulation in many passages so that the cellist can hear the orchestra clearly at all times. This was especially necessary in the first movement where the orchestral writing is somewhat amorphous at times, presenting a challenge for this format where the cellist will necessarily have to follow the orchestra. What we have created in the minus versions is a compromise between realism and faithfulness to the score on the one hand, and playability on the other: when in doubt we have erred on the side of playability.

Best wishes for lots of fun! There is nothing quite like the thrill of playing with full symphony orchestra!

Nancy Green and Stephen Ware

(For British players: eighth note = quaver, quarter note = crotchet)

Édouard Lalo

VIOLONCELLO CONCERTO IN D MINOR

C O N T E N T S

Édouard Lalo
Violoncello Concerto in D minor
A son ami Adolphe Fischer
Composed in 1877

Violoncello solo

Edited by Nancy Green

Prélude
Lento

Violoncello solo

6

Violoncello solo

Violoncello solo

Violoncello solo

Violoncello solo

Violoncello solo

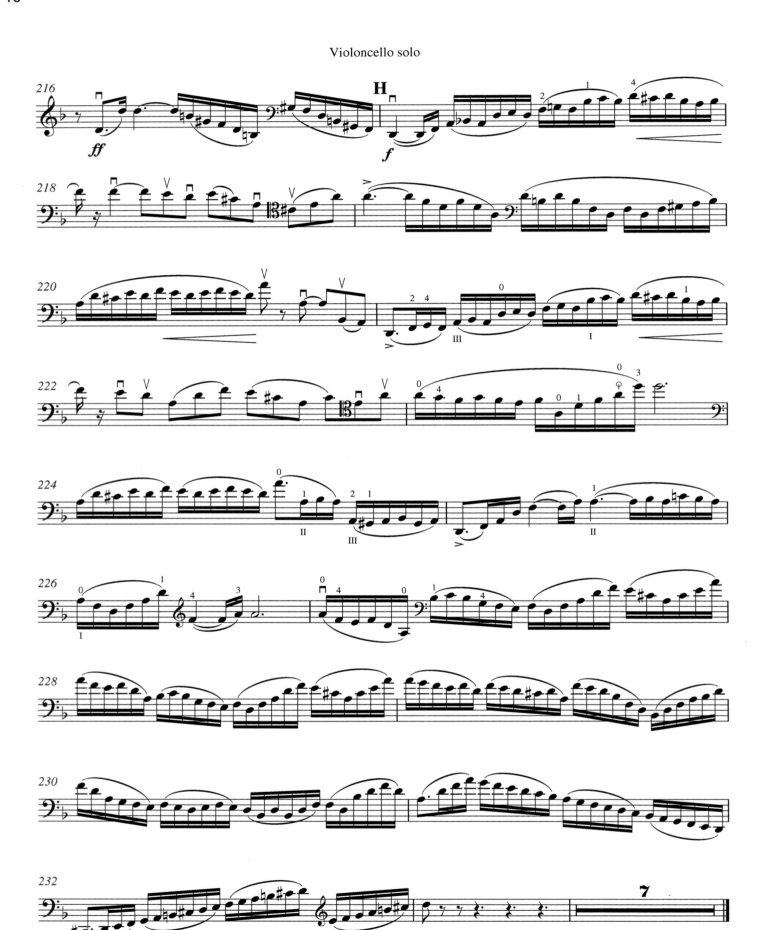

Violoncello solo

Intermezzo

Andantino con moto ♩. = 58

Violoncello solo

Violoncello solo

Introduction

Violoncello solo

Violoncello solo

Violoncello solo

Violoncello solo

Violoncello solo

A World of Violoncello Music from Music Minus One
Quality Accompaniment Editions since 1950
www.musicminusone.com

Chamber Classics

BEETHOVEN Complete Violoncello Sonatas (7 CDs) ....MMO CD 3755
BEETHOVEN Trios 8 in Eb & 11 in G..MMO CD 3710
BEETHOVEN Quartet A min, op.132 ....MMO CD 3713
BEETHOVEN Son. A, op. 69; TELEMANN 'Cello Duet B-flat ....MMO CD 3715
DVORAK Quintet A maj, op. 81 ....MMO CD 3714
MENDELSSOHN Trio No. 1 in d, op. 49; No. 2 in c, op. 66......................MMO CD 3754
RACHMANINOV Son. Vcl./Piano, op. 19 ....MMO CD 3731
RAVEL Trio in A min (Vardi Trio) ....MMO CD 3707
SCHUBERT Quintet A, op. 114, 'Trout'...MMO CD 3721
SCHUBERT Trio B-flat maj, op. 99 (A.Shulman) (2 CD)...........................MMO CD 3711
SCHUBERT Trio E-flat maj, op. 100 (A.Shulman) (2 CD) ....MMO CD 3712
SCHUMANN Trio No. 1 D min, op. 63 (D.Miller) ....MMO CD 3709
Ten Concert Pieces for 'Cello and Piano (K.Dillingham) ....MMO CD 3704
Cello Soloist: Classic Solos (S.Thomas) Best seller!................................MMO CD 3726

Inspirational Classics

Christmas Memories ....MMO CDG 1203

Instrumental Classics with Orchestra

C.P.E. BACH Conc. A min, Wq170/H432 (Chanteux/Stuttgart) ....MMO CD 3702
BOCCHERINI Conc.9 Bb; BRUCH Kol Nidrei (Chant./Stuttgart) ....MMO CD 3703
BRAHMS Double A min, op. 102 (Kouzmanova/Groh) (3 CD) ....MMO CD 3722
DVORAK Conc. B min, op.104 (Lawson/Stuttgart) (2 CD).........................MMO CD 3701
ELGAR Conc. E min, op. 85 (Krastev/Plodoiv) (2 CD) ....MMO CD 3720
HAYDN Conc. C maj, HobVIIb:1 ....MMO CD 3718
HAYDN Conc. D maj, HobVIIb:2 (Wiszniowski/Plovdiv) ....MMO CD 3719
EDUARDO LALO Cello Concerto (Nancy Green) ....MMO CD 3780
SAINT-SAENS: Concerto No. 1 in A (Nancy Green) ....MMO CD 3779
SCHUMANN Conc. A min, op. 129 ....MMO CD 3705
TCHAIKOVSKY Variations on Rococo Theme ....MMO CD 3773
WINER Conc.SCHUBERT Ave Maria; SAINT-SAENS Allegro Appass ......MMO CD 3716

Jazz, Standards and Big Band

BOLLING 'Cello Suite with Jazz Trio..(Lawson,Gross,Burrows) ....MMO CD 3706
Great Scott! Ragtime Minus You...(Zinn's Ragtime Qt.) ....MMO CD 3708

MUSIC MINUS ONE
50 Executive Boulevard • Elmsford, New York 10523-1325
914-592-1188 • e-mail: info@musicminusone.com
www.musicminusone.com

MMO 3780

ISBN 978-0-9916347-5-0